T0208160

LOVE: When It Hurts So Bad But It Feels So Good

Real talk on love, relationships and becoming a better you

Amber Shanel

authorHOUSE®

AuthorHouse™ LLC
1663 Liberty Drive
Bloomington, IN 47403
www.authorhouse.com
Phone: 1-800-839-8640

Published by AuthorHouse 05/08/2014

ISBN: 978-1-4969-0484-3 (sc)
ISBN: 978-1-4969-0483-6 (e)

Library of Congress Control Number: 2014906955

Any people depicted in stock imagery provided by Thinkstock are models,
and such images are being used for illustrative purposes only.
Certain stock imagery © Thinkstock.

This book is printed on acid-free paper.

Because of the dynamic nature of the Internet, any web addresses or
links contained in this book may have changed since publication and
may no longer be valid. The views expressed in this work are solely those
of the author and do not necessarily reflect the views of the publisher,
and the publisher hereby disclaims any responsibility for them.

I dedicate this book to the loves of my life: my sons Nasjir and Carmelo. You are the reason I do what I do. Looking at your amazing smiles each day gives me purpose. You inspire me to be the best mom I can be and a reflection of your love. I hope to make you proud.

Let my determination motivate you to be the best you can be. Unique and valuable to me, you are worth all the greatness life has to give. You are my kings!

Mommy loves you always.

Acknowledgments

First and foremost I have to say thank you to my Creator, the one who has blessed me with the vision, ideas, and opportunity to make this book a reality. Through God, *all* things are possible!

Next, I would like to acknowledge someone I have never met but who has been influential in my life since fifth grade: Maya Angelou. Ever since I recited the poems "And Still I Rise" and "Phenomenal Woman," I knew that writing would be a part of my life forever. Her poetry has given me strength and made me proud to be a woman. Thank you, Maya Angelou, for being that voice.

I would like to thank all my family and friends who believed in me and never doubted my success.

Amber Shanel

Contents

Introduction

Why do we gamble with our hearts, playing Russian roulette with our emotions?

We know the risk of getting hurt, but we still want to be in love so bad! Sometimes, because of how intense our passion is, being in love can hurt, but yet it feels so good. There are ups and there are downs. Many times, we gravitate to the great feeling of ecstasy that love brings at its best and ignore the alternative.

So why does it hurt so bad? Giving someone your all is like bungee jumping—either way, you will fall. Whether you fall in love or out, your emotions can go to an all-time high. You can shed tears of joy or you can weep flowing streams of heartbreak. Giving your all means making yourself completely vulnerable and transparent in hopes that your unveiling will be rewarded with **gratitude**, **acceptance**, and the ultimate achievement, **commitment**.

Sometimes in the pursuit of what you *think* you want, your vision gets clouded by being naive and lack of self-identity. In this book, I capture a very real and honest perspective on love and relationships. I give revelation and understanding on such topics as trust, real love, and when to let go. You will be amazed at how you relate to some of the eye-opening topics described in this book. You will definitely be asking yourself, "How did it come to this?"

The reality is that no one is perfect, and sometimes in the game of love, relationships are truly tested. Ultimately, you will find that after the great journey of self-discovery through life's ups and downs, you live and you learn.

Part 1

Expressions of Love

Your love lasts like a sweet scent of thanksgiving dinner
Your smile touches my spirit and warms my soul
Your kiss, gentle, making my heart long for more
A glass of passion I kneel over to pour
An alluring whisper of loves menacing rhythms
A riddle of curiosity our minds intertwined
Your eyes speaking of constant pleasure to be united as one
Together, our given family future goals to come
I love to stare at your face, handsome and calm
Speaking love, determination and faith
You, my soul mate no one else could contemplate
What we've grown to become over this journey of years
A love full of compassion and devotion to care

Love vs. Infatuation: How Do You Know When It's Real?

"The part that bothered me the most was if he really truly cared about me, or if it was all a big lie. I know he cared. I think he did give me more (love) than he intended to . . ."

This is part of a text I received early one morning from a close friend named Jasmine. The day before, she had discovered that her boyfriend was still seeing his ex-girlfriend. Disappointed, embarrassed, and upset, she confided to me about someone she thought she was in love with. But was he in love with her? It seems simple to imply that based on his actions, he was not in love. If it is that simple to suggest, then why do people use the word *love*? Most times, people **just don't know how to love right**.

To me, someone who loves you should respect, appreciate, and care about your well-being. Infatuation seems to be more of an exaggerated feeling of love. It is superficial, without substance.

So ladies, are you in love or infatuated?

Ladies, why do you think you are in love? Could it be that you are in love with the idea of being in love?

There are many times throughout my life that I was infatuated, but there is no way that could have been love! I remember feeling "so complete." It's funny how easy it is for us to say we are in love simply because someone shows interest in us. Is that all it takes? Sometimes, yes. And ladies, in case you didn't know, the fellas already know this valid truth!

Many times, we gravitate to the idea of being in love. You see how it is romanticized on television all the time— gazing in each other's eyes for hours, being serenaded while having a candlelit dinner on the rooftop, rose petals gently flowing in the wind as the man and woman meet. All the makings of love. (LOL, for all you texters!) This definitely sets the mood and atmosphere for love to linger. But what are the actions that persuade you to fall for someone? It has to be something significant that they did or said that made you feel compelled to love them. If a sense of affection was created strictly on physical attraction, is that really love or infatuation? You know when someone says they fell in love at first sight . . . Do people really meet and fall in love at first sight? I think it begins as an infatuation that can grow into love for that person.

Let's discover what men and woman really want . . .

Made to last

Just like feelings run high, speeding fast
I wanna know gotta know what it takes to make it last
A thought, a glance, an emotion a song
A moment infatuation desired too long
Making someone stay, a luxury to a hearts beat
Feeling wanted, admired a yearning to keep
Wondered by many asked by a few
Made to last casually means starting over new

Men vs. Women

I did a survey asking men and women what they look for in a partner and what they expect in a relationship. Based on the results, both males and females were looking for very similar qualities. One guy expressed how he needed a mate who was supportive, respectful, open-minded, faithful, and loving. A young lady described someone who was ambitious, driven, passionate, humorous, trustworthy, reliable, and patient. Not too much to ask for, right? The common factor in most of the responses was someone who was supportive and trustworthy. If men and women want similar qualities in their mates, then why does there seem to be so much mis-communication?

Each person has unique characteristics. These form the essence of who we are as individuals. I think what causes unrealistic expectations and setbacks in a relationship is not accepting people for who they are. If when you met your boyfriend he was a momma's boy, how can you expect him not to be? If when he met you, you were reserved and not really into crowds, what gives him the right to complain if you do not want to go to social settings every weekend? Your main goal should not be to mold your significant other to be who you want them to be! Instead, it is better to support them and encourage their strengths. Try not to focus on their weaknesses.

Realizing if there are unsettling qualities that you cannot ignore is the deal breaker to whether this is really the match for you. Now in a committed relationship, compromise and growth are important. At some point, there should be progress. As time goes by, you are changing, and so are your needs. The key to evolving is that you both experience the growth and maturity together.

Simple Love

Simple love is spontaneous a constant pleasure
Humor subsiding any feeling of awkwardness
A popcorn fight
A snowball thrown at your head
A pajama wrestling match before you go to bed
The quiet walks in the park
The questions of your past
The inevitable suggestion that this simple love will last
Male and females flirting with the mysterious answer to loves
menacing riddles
Teasing their curiosity with secrecy and content
Long lasting love is an emotion worth striving

Love: Is It Really That Simple?

Why do we long to be in a relationship? What is the deep attraction to belonging to another person? Barack and Michelle Obama and Jada and Will Smith are examples of inspiring couples. They appear to be forces when they are together. There is something amazing about a power couple. We all want to know more about the dynamics of their bond. They exemplify the meaning of true love. Yes, ladies it actually does exist! Each duo complements each other, supporting, uplifting, and bringing out each other's best.

Marriage is presented as a way to join as one working unit. So how do they make it work? What is the blueprint for a thriving relationship? One quality I've noticed about winning couples is they view their lives as a joint venture. They work as a team. At times in relationships, individuals can become complacent. No longer do they view their soul mate as their best friend. No longer are they viewed as their soul mate. Now this person is perceived as a roommate, a convenience, a dependent, and sometimes even a liability. Rather than planning enchanting, meaningful moments together, each person is navigating their space, time, and energy apart. A relationship is like a loving partnership. Happy couples that I have witnessed find common interests that will keep them communicating and seeking each other's support. Spending time together is awesome when you look forward to it.

Finding someone you are compatible with, who shares similar views on life, love, and relationships, can be like looking for a job—it's hard work! Like a huge puzzle, it is essential that the pieces fit just right in order to be complete. I think when there is a real connection, it is like a magnetic bond that cannot be forced or imitated; you just feel it.

Although compatibility can alleviate some stress, even in the best relationships there are challenges. We all have our own ways of thinking. I know it's hard to believe, but your man actually had a life before he met you! You both have different life experiences. Learning to adjust to each other's personality takes time. At times, you get frustrated and wish there was a return policy for a connection gone wrong. As you develop as a person, you realize what attracts you and what pushes you away. What you will tolerate and what you will not. Women, you have to know your breaking point. Some relationships are truly a test. Some tests are to enlighten and strengthen you in order to develop your character. Love is the key factor to knowing if it is all worth it. In the test of love, will you pass or will you fail?

Too Anxious

The touch the feel the smell the taste
Wanting the receiving the impurity embraced
A new friend new beginning new adventure new skills
Old traps old raps old persuasion old thrills
Could have waited but didn't
So grown so naïve
Easily misguided too easily deceived
Young children curious so anxious to know
Discovering, experiencing, expectations become low
Finding out what should have taken time to understand
Too soon a woman, too late a man
Purity and innocence no longer their prime essence
The deception of lust one of their new found lessons
Regret? Uncertainty? Mixed emotions not put to a cessation
Reality, consequences, the cause of no desired duration
Too soon too high too free too late
No thought
No consideration
No intention
No debate
Was it worth it? Acting all wild, mentally prematurely conceiving a child
Criticism, scrutiny, labeling can hurt
Don't cry don't worry just value your self worth
To the young man who arrogantly walks away like you never played a part
Pretending that it's the end little do you know it's just a start

To the young girl so incredulous that it would happen to you
There's sex intercourse which one did you do?
　　Cause either way it's all the same, many different styles but
only one name
Can explain, what has turned you to this direction
The feeling, thriving, feigning for affection
Just like the young man you both had choices to make
Curiosity, pleasure, eagerness a mistake?
Life settling acceptance to learn
No longer an obstacle
No longer your turn

You Have No Idea!

One of the best articles I have ever read was by a woman named Marlene Fernandez. It said,

"We should watch who we choose to even spend one afternoon, evening, or day, with why? Because our feelings and emotions begin to get involved and before we know it-one thing leads to another. Our own values and standards start to get lost in the power of influence that others can have on us. Many times people ended up in the wrong relationships, friendships, marriages, with the wrong person—just because they spent one afternoon, date, etcetera with someone who wasn't really a person they should have been with in the first place. When looking for mates or even friends for that matter do we realize that a person's actions and attitudes are a direct reflection of what is in their heart? Do you realize that the choices we make as to who we associate with are a direct reflection of what is in our hearts? How many times have people found themselves involved in situations or actions with people that they never imagined themselves to be involved with? Caught up in situations that are very hard to get out of."

She mentioned that choosing the company we keep is an image of us as well. Take a look at the people you associate with. What kind of people are you attracting? Do you notice a pattern of always being interested in the wrong type of men? These are things to think about. What are their direct actions telling you about what is really in their hearts?

Just Want to be Loved

Just want to be loved
An appreciated touch
A loose fitting lace skirt admired too much
A soft sensation tingling emotions go deep
Memories flowing streams of passion to keep

Giving Your Love Away

So it's a cold Saturday night and you're home alone with huge rollers parading all over your head and rainbow-colored nightgown on. The room is dim and you're slouched on your couch, shoveling spoonfuls of French-vanilla ice cream into your mouth while your eyes are locked attentively to the television screen. You increase the volume as Meagan Good storms out of her boyfriend's apartment after she realizes she was tricked into giving up the "cookie"! You're watching the movie *Think Like a Man* and it has you glued to the screen. Lonely, you start to think about yourself . . . Do you find yourself giving your love away because you're feeling lonely? Calling someone you usually would not even spend half a breath speaking to just because you know they're available? You are feeling alone and just want to be loved.

Having sex is the single-most intimate form of affection. It creates a connection, a giving of yourself. This is the one moment you can be most vulnerable. You are giving someone access to a sacred part of you—your body. Many believe intercourse goes way beyond the physical; it affects their mind and their soul. Perception is so important. What you perceive as reality becomes your reality. When you feel intimacy, you give meaning to your relationship based on that. Or you might not even be involved, but now you feel like you are. Your emotions are now involved. You believe this man feels the same connection you do. The reality is he may be thinking the complete opposite! Sex is very powerful. It will take a friendship to another level. It will build feelings that were not previously there.

Do not confuse having sex with making love. It is so easy to give your love away. I believe intimacy has purpose. I do not want to give my goods to someone who does not deserve it! Women, our bodies are valuable, and when it comes to this, we are in control. Know your worth! I suggest persuading a man to make love to your mind. Have great conversation; draw your attention. **This is what separates the boys from the men**. Yes, we all have desires, but do not allow yourself to be used. Wouldn't it be great to connect and build a love for each other in which sex is just an added bonus? That's what I want—to experience the full effects of falling in love with the person I'm involved with. Allow a man to remove layers. No, I'm not talking about clothing! I'm talking about removing the layers to get to your heart. Getting to know the real you beyond the superficial. Do not underestimate the depth of your personality and uniqueness. You are an original. You may not be all that deep, but consider yourself a woman of substance. There is something about you unlike anyone else. If a man can stay interested and intrigued by you without being physically involved, I believe that shows that he loves you for you. Who you are, your personality, your motives, and your abilities are what should separate you from any other women, not your performance in bed! For me, a committed relationship, a marriage, is a union deserving of all I have to give.

Playing the Leading Role

"In the middle of a heated argument he said something I never thought he would say to me "we were never together". SMH. I told him that was a low blow and he didn't have to say that to me. I swore that I would never contact him again, never wanted to hear from him again and I meant it."

I had to start this chapter with a text I received from a friend concerning a conversation she had with her "man." Can you believe it? He said the four words a female dreads to hear: "We were never together." Is there a way to tell if you were ever really in a relationship? Imagine you're dating someone, you feel comfortable and confident with where this is going, and in the midst of an argument you two are having, he informs you that it was never so. I can only imagine how emotionally frustrating it must have been, for him to renounce what my friend believed had a firm foundation.

Why would he use that choice of words to pierce her heart? Was it to relieve his conscience of any wrongdoing he had done? I am not a therapist, but I do know that words hurt, especially when it comes to rejection. As women, many times when a man says one thing, we read into it on a-whole-nother level. Most of us definitely dissect a man's words to understand what he is really saying.

Now, not only are you realizing that he never really felt committed to you as you felt to him, but your mind is clouded with thoughts of why he suddenly doesn't want to commit or claim you. When did he start feeling like this, or was he ever being genuine to you at all? It creates a ripple effect of confusion, misunderstanding, and emotional distress.

He may apologize later on that day and think nothing of his negligent description of what "this is." Not aware of the corrupt seed he has now planted, which may infect the basis of your situation. **If a man feels as though you are not together, then what are you?** You are whatever you allow him to define it as. If he is able to continue to carry on with relationship privileges without the actual commitment, why would he bother to actually commit? It is like collecting unemployment. He's not actually working, but he is receiving all the benefits, bonuses, and incentives without being on the job. He also has the freedom to post his résumé (Facebook and Instagram) to find a job that is suitable. It's a grace period. You both are weighing your options in case a better opportunity comes along, and there's nothing wrong with that because you two are single! He's not your man!

The misunderstanding comes along when you *assume* that, because you are playing the role of his girlfriend or wife, this is what he has subliminally agreed to as well. This is so far from reality. Never assume; communication is the key. There needs to be a mutually spoken agreement of what you're building toward. This is so important mainly because nine times out of ten, feelings are involved. You never want to mislead someone when it comes to their emotions. Trust me: I have been heartbroken a few times and although I find strength to recover and move on, it never takes away from the severity of the pain at that moment. It still hurts.

Maybe you are comfortable with him not being your man. You say, "We know what we have is real and it does not have to be defined." As long as you are comfortable with knowing your role in his life and willing to play your position, that is fine. That may not work for everyone. You have to know what your expectations and standards are as well as what you are willing to accept. **Most importantly, be aware of what your heart can handle.**

A Woman's Intuition: Be Wise Not Naïve

I've always believed that I was able to detect when something wasn't right in any given situation. My son would call it the spidey sense. It's a feeling you just can't shake. So imagine you are in a relationship, whether dating or married, yet something just does not feel right. You have some reservations about how honest your mate is being. This feeling, instinct, or emotion is better known as a woman's intuition. Now some might judge you as being insecure. And maybe you are, but you have this gut feeling that something is not right. My motto is be wise, not naïve.

When you're in a commitment, I do not suggest you look for or expect the worse from your mate, but always be wise. Trust yourself before you trust anyone else. Trust yourself to know how you should be treated. **Know what you expect love to look like**. Does love to you resemble being passive, possessive, and deceiving? It shouldn't. You are supposed to be his partner. Whether you are his girlfriend or his wife, having a title does not give anyone the right to treat you any less than you deserve. Some may say, "Oh well. If he didn't love me, he would not have made me his girlfriend." Is that what he has to do for you to disregard your requirements of him as your man? Give you a title? Actions speak louder than words. If someone says, "I miss you" but rarely spends quality time with you, their actions are proving the opposite of what they are saying. **Remember, what someone does is a direct reflection of what is in their heart.** It's important to say what you mean and mean what you say. Or like Tihari from *Love and Hip Hop* would say, "Show and prove!"

I think women are very intelligent, but most of us feed off of emotions. If your partner is sending off signals that he is not in tune with you or interested the way he once was, that can send off an alarm. I've noticed that at times, it is very hard for men to hide a secret; they leave hints everywhere. Most women tend to be very intuitive to changes in habits, such as daily routines and mannerisms. I am known for reading between the lines. It's like a subliminal message. Women notice if all of a sudden their man gets dressed up to go over his friend's house or is out later in the night than usual. Communication is vital, because without it, there is room for assumption.

Women, you cannot read your man's mind, and you do not want to assume! When your woman's intuition is in action, be wise and not naïve. If you truly trust your partner, believe that if you express your concerns he will be open and honest with you. Give him the benefit of a doubt before taking any further measures.

Part 2

When It Hurts So Bad But It Feels So Good

I pause to reminisce on how it felt to cry
The pain subsiding tears fail to deny
A piece of me shattered and frail
Envying hearts that were over looked by betrayal
A moment of content a sigh of relief
As my heart beat rhythms faster at each serenading lie
Sounds so sweet
Gentle Kisses make me blush
A feeling of happiness a desire to trust
In love once again
Heart ache in reserve
This feeling, my hearts destination
An emotion so high
Lets try again
Lets get it right
When it hurts so bad but it feels so good

Lauren Hill said it best. "When it hurts so bad, why's it feel so good?" Being in love can take you on a roller-coaster ride. Although you don't want to experience the fall, you can't resist staying on as you elevate with excitement. The flow of emotions is like a natural high: you desperately want it to never end so you look for ways to get it back. It just feels so good! There are those who are fortunate enough to experience the highs without the lows.

So often, we gamble with our heart, playing Russian roulette with our emotions. We know the risk of getting hurt, but we still want to be in love so bad! Many times, we gravitate to the great feeling of ecstasy that love brings at its best and ignore the alternative.

At times, a relationship can start to unravel right before your eyes and you're left wondering, *How did it come to this?* The reality is that no one is perfect, and sometimes in the game of love, relationships are truly tested. Here's an example of someone who when faced with a *love crisis* was truly driven by their emotions . . .

To Spy or Not to Spy: How to Monitor Your Man's Calls

Warning: if you have to resort to this extent to expose what you suspect, then it is necessary to reevaluate your relationship!

Stefanie-

Red or black Stefanie thought to herself as she drift past the colorful collection of phones. The phone store was unusually vacant, which allowed Stefanie ample time to be indecisive. "I don't know?" she mumbled unsure if she should purchase the phone at all. She suddenly noticed a for-sale label clearly in her view, $100 off. "That's the one!" She chanted, as her eager fingers collapsed around the mobile device. "Great choice!" the customer service rep implied, as Stefanie swiped her debit card. The dimple on her cheek deepened as each muscle on her face stretched to expose her illuminating smile. Building up was a sensation of hidden joy and excitement. She couldn't wait to get home.

Running playfully to her silver BMW, she clamped the door handle with her cold fingers and swung the door open with force. She then fervently slid into the seats leather interior and tore open the box, lifting up the phone for display. Energized, she decided not to wait to get to her destination to open it. "Such a nice gift" she thought, pleased with her selection. She quickly rambled through the phone apps to find a spy monitor to download. "Perfect!" There was one with access that was undetectable. She couldn't wait to give her generous gift to her man . . .

First of all, let's be honest. Regardless of how confident you may be, I believe everyone has been curious of their partner's phone activity. Although you may want to know about your mate's intentions or motives, obsession over it is not a healthy emotion. It causes you to be consumed, like an addiction. Who wants to pursue an untrustworthy relationship like that? Consider an honest relationship that has potential. There are so many other things in life that deserve your effort, energy, and attention.

Do You Really Want to Know the Truth? (The Truth Will Set You Free)

Although this may not have been the best way to find out the truth, Stefanie needed to know. She was becoming increasingly tired and aggravated with Chellos deception when something was clearly not being said. Once Stefanie handed Chello the phone she was ready to find out the truth. Ever heard the saying the truth will set you free? Well I don't know about that, but it will definitely take you to a place of no return. "Happy birthday bae" Stefanie chimed as she presented the neatly wrapped lavender gift box. "Aww thanks Stef" Chello weakly replied as he nudged his head for her to give him a kiss. "Your welcome bae" she whispered lazily, accepting his feeble form of gratitude.

Once she returned home she hesitantly entered her room to access her spy monitor account on her computer. As she swung herself in the cushioned seat at the small desk she quickly entered the password, anticipation increasing. The rhythmic tapping of Stefanie's foot against the wooden floor began to fade and drift to mute. As though she had seen a horrific sight, she quickly turned away from the monitor in disbelief. Is this really happening? She took a deep breath, hallucinating a dull pain in her chest, as suddenly it felt hard to breathe. Although she had known the warning signs, Stefanie would not allow herself to accept that Chello would convincingly deceive her—until now.

As she stared wearily at the screen she saw the incoming and outgoing calls and text messages from Chellos phone. The first call he made once he got the phone was to the female Stefanie suspected he was dealing with. This was undeniable being that the girl text at least 5 photos to him within an hour of him getting the phone in his possession! "This chick is ridiculous!" Stefanie thought, as she clicked and viewed each photo. As she clicked on each photo, a tingling numbness began to radiate along her finger tip. "She's not even cute!" Stefanie moaned disgusted with this whole affair.

Click clack click clack! Stefanie's 4 inch heels pierced the floor as she paced back and forth across the dim room. Shaking her head as her hands overlapped her tear saturated eyes, she attempted to wipe the streams of salty water from her mascara painted cheek in vain. "How could he?" She sobbed, motioning herself to calm down and breathe. As she in haled and exhaled deeply, her mind was clouded with shadowy images of the girl's silhouette. "But he said she's just a friend," a phrase kept ringing through Stefanie's mind like a bad anthem. This is what he insisted to Stefanie, when approached 2 months ago responding to her woman's intuition.

"I was a fool to believe his lies!" Stefanie disputed as she glared at the menacing computer screen. "What to do, what to do, what to do now?" she contemplated hopelessly. "But he said she's just a friend" is what began to resonate as she climbed into bed and laid in fetal position. She silently drifted off to sleep, escaping feelings of betrayal and regret.

Trust: Is It Overrated?

Is it naïve to put so much trust in your partner if it results in them disappointing you? I do not think so. Even though you should guard yourself at times, it's hard to be comfortable if you do not trust the authenticity of your mutual love. When I'm in a relationship, I want to give my all. If I am unable to do that, what's point of being in one? To cheat is a violation of that trust.

In order to cheat, there has to have been an agreement of expectations and boundaries. For someone to syndicate their love to another person is unfair. Once you agree to be trusting and faithful, you are held accountable. The irony to this whole concept of trust in Stefanie's case is that she trusted Chello even when her gut feeling made her question the validity of him and his friendship with that female. It wasn't until Stefanie faced the physical evidence that confirmed her worst fears. **When you search for the truth, you have to be prepared for whatever it may be.**

A Broken Heart

*Slash! Ripped pages, crumbled thoughts filtered in a memory
filled breeze*
How could you! Penetrates like a sharp cupids arrow
Pain possessing what love should have restored
A frail heart, jaded by such evident neglect
Feelings itching to be released, buried and decade
Seeking a life massage to ease the mental distress
Silence
Peace
Poetic rhythms scribble a flow to a new beat
A new beginning simple yet complex
*Clear clouds reverse dried tears on a painted cheek with smudged
mascara*
Sunny skies
A new breeze shattering blended memories of betrayal

I Broke the Windows out Your Car: Revenge, Is it Worth It?

Stefanie-

Clash!!! An echo of glass shattering effortlessly, as a brick massages its surface. Stefanie, with intensity jumps in place in the cold dark drive way. "Ha!" She hit the car window. Her boyfriend Chello peaked out of the apartment window frozen in shock! "How did it come to this?" Stefanie shouted at him with a fierce tone, swaying her hands casually back and forth, conveying her satisfaction. As her one sided conversation came to a dismissal, the horror-struck expression on Chellos face proved he should have thought twice before breaking her heart. As she glanced at the casualty, his "hoes" beat down Honda, she walked away with thoughts running involuntarily through her mind. Revenge . . . is it worth it?

Most women are emotional individuals. Many of us view statements such as "I love you" literally, as it should be intended to be said with sincerity. Everyone has heard the phrase "It's a thin line between love and hate." Well, that is so true! Play with someone's emotions and they get all out of character. Now they are focused on revenge.

Now Stefanie definitely took her actions to the extreme when finding out the truth. In no way do I condone this method of resolution, but I do feel her pain. A year after this incident, Stefanie still possessed feelings of regret and humiliation for retaliating in such a public display of anger. So revenge, is it worth it? I'm not going to sit here and give you a textbook answer. At the moment, I'm sure Stefanie felt great! But that was only for a moment. The emotional damage from being heartbroken would still remain, only now would she have to endure the pain and embarrassment of what she did as well.

His Perspective

Viewing the situation from his point of view, I do not think he regretted what he did but rather that it was exposed. He may have felt a sporadic sense of remorse after witnessing Stefanie's heartache extending through that glass window! But why should it take something like that to go so wrong in order for him to get it right? It's like when you watch those shows on television when the bad guy gets away for a while, but eventually he always gets caught. Why do the bad guys think their tactics of escaping are any more impressive than the others before them? Most times, it's due to the smaller defiant acts that they did prior to the larger ones. They got away with smaller acts, which led up to the larger ones and then the grand finale. That's when the curtain closes and the show is over. The same scenario can be applied to a relationship.

"Being Too Understanding under the Wrong Circumstances."

Before thunder, there is lightning. Before ice, there is rain. In any extreme event, there are signs leading up to its appearance. **At times, people are so busy waiting for major violations in a relationship that they ignore the minor ones.** Unfortunately, these small violations pave the way for the larger ones. If you allow someone to disrespect you, you have just given permission to be disrespected again. It becomes repetitive, each time becoming more and more excessive. My friend Jasmine once told me her downfall was being **too understanding under the wrong circumstances.** There are certain boundaries as a woman you cannot allow to be crossed, no matter how loving and kind you are. Kindness can easily be manipulated and used as a weakness. The condition of all relationships is diverse, yet there has to be at least one common ground. In any case, once it becomes physical or verbal abuse, there is no room for understanding. Your safety and well-being are now being compromised. Seek healthy relationships.

Silence: Is It the Best Policy?

Remember my friend in chapter 1, Jasmine, who found out her man was seeing his ex-girlfriend? Well, this is the complete text that she sent me.

"So I've been thinking . . . a lot! And I realize it's embarrassing to her relationship as well that he's bringing me around his close friends. I mean that says some things about their relationship too. I've been feeling like the loser in all of this but I'm not. It's his lost. And for her sake I hope she doesn't find out his extracurricular activities. He should be lucky it was me because anyone else would have brought it to her door step. He's a great negotiator and can talk people into understanding things and he uses that in business and his personal relationships. And I'm sure the real him will come out eventually. Maybe she knows how to handle him, and if so great for them. But I know why my gut tells me to ignore him, because after what he did to me he doesn't even deserve my friendship. He abused my kindness and generosity and called it dumbness and stupidity. The part that bothered me the most was if he really truly cared about me, or if it was all a big lie. I know he cared, I think he did give me more then he intended to. But he made that all irrelevant because he was so selfish. He cared about his happiness and keeping me around, more than my happiness and letting me go. There I think that explains it all! lol I feel better already. Bottom line, he's the loser and I shouldn't be mad at

myself. He's great at what he does. I just know I have got to get great at spotting B.S. and calling people out on it and moving on . . ."

At this point, Jasmine was done dealing with her unfaithful boyfriend and had come to terms with it. Now she viewed the whole situation differently. She even went as far as to admit that he was good at what he does, but that she had to be wiser at discerning. By texting me, she was able to get it all off her chest. I was glad that she had decided not to be the victim but to realize it was his loss. She had done nothing to deserve being deceived by him.

For a week, he called and called and called Jasmine. But she resisted the urge to respond. She had decided that silence was the best policy.

So ladies, do you agree? Is silence the best policy? I think Jasmine was very intuitive of her own weaknesses. She knew that just hearing the faintest whisper of his deep, familiar, serenading voice would make her vulnerable. Jasmine knew it would make her question herself. *Did he really mean to hurt me? Maybe it's not that big of a deal.* These thoughts would stampede through her mind. Sometimes, it is necessary to **shut your feelings off** for a while. Picture yourself on the outside of the dilemma looking in. How does the situation look now?

Part 3

Saying Good-bye

Saying goodbye is never easy
Saying goodbye so long
Tears overshadow faded grinning
Sighs of unhappiness prolonged
Saying goodbye to a friend so familiar like the air you breathe each day
Knowing after this moment all things will be different
Emotions fading away
Goodbye to my first love, partner and friend
Goodbye to our past joys
Goodbye to a future not promised but so desperately hoped for
I wish you the best because you are worth the best God has to give
Knowing after this test we will both overcome the greatest obstacle . . .
To forgive

One of the hardest things I ever had to do in my life was let go. Letting go of something I was fighting so hard to keep. To say good-bye to "a future not promised but so desperately hoped for" feels like you're giving up on everything you ever knew and understood. All I knew was me and this man. Regardless of all that we had been through in our relationship, I hadn't pictured my life any other way.

Rebuild or Let It Go?

When devastation occurs, you feel like your whole world has been turned upside down. "After the storm," you have to decide whether to rebuild or let it go. I believe that every couple encounters obstacles. How you deal with them defines the significance of your bond. In marriage, you vow to stay together through good times and bad. You have to decide if there is a chance for reconciliation. You have to decide if it is worth it. Are you and your partner willing to work it out? Will the necessary changes be done? Will you accept the relationship if things do not change? This is one thing only you can decide, but always consider if your needs are being met. When in the relationship are there times where you feel you partner builds you up? Or are they constantly breaking you down? **Any person has the ability to change, but they have to want to.**

The Healing Process

Whether you decide to reconcile or let it go, you still are in need of healing. **Healing is a process.** This is a process that truly helped me to deal with my own emotional issues. It was just my way of dealing with the transition of leaving all that I knew and starting over. I hope it will encourage and inspire you all as well.

The first step is becoming committed to yourself. You have to love yourself before anyone else can! You set the standards on how you want to be treated. People only do what you allow them to. A way to prove that you love yourself is by allowing the opportunity to heal. Once you truly love yourself and are ready to heal, the next step is to learn from your experiences.

Learning from experiences is not to make you feel like a failure but a process that teaches, motivates, and empowers you to overcome any other obstacle s that may arise. It's like discovering the answers to a test you didn't pass. You already know the possible outcome if duplicating the same strategy. This time, concentrate, strengthen your weaknesses, and pass that test! Gain wisdom and become a better you!

When healing, it's okay to acknowledge feelings of hurt, anger, or even shame, but you do not want a negative experience to leave a residue of bitterness and hostility in your heart. My friend Jasmine confided to me that she felt embarrassed and ashamed. She had allowed her boyfriend to make her look and feel foolish. She ignored the warning signs in hopes that he would "know better." Becoming a better you entails finding peace, love, and a positive attitude regardless of the circumstances around you.

The next step is acceptance. Accept the things you have no control over. The hardest thing to accept is that the person who hurt you may never apologize or have feelings of remorse. Regardless how they feel, you have a responsibility to yourself to find peace. Even if you were wrong, you have to accept it and move on. Claim it, learn from it, and move forward. Make positive decisions in the areas of your life you are able to control, such as your friends and how you spend your time and energy. If you know that going to a particular restaurant or public setting will cause bad memories or even an unexpected encounter with your ex, then don't go there! Do not put yourself in a compromising situation that may leave you vulnerable or in a position of rejection. Also, understand that sometimes you cannot take it personally. I know that might sound insensitive, but more than likely, you were not the first, nor will you be the last person that gets mistreated. That person just may not know how to treat women in general. **Accepting who they are helps you realize the type of person you are not—and what you will not tolerate.**

The next step is to forgive. Forgiveness is for your benefit. Forgiveness allows you the ability to let go of those damaging emotions. Release the pain; embrace happiness and another chance to get it right. I like to say, "Let go and let God." When I went through my own personal heartbreak, the only way I was able to gain peace and perspective was through prayer. I remember one of my best friends commending me for healing and finding peace so quickly. She was like, "Girl, what took me a year to do only took you a few months!" I must say it definitely was a process and did go through all the emotions, but I was able to find comfort and peace through God. I was able to let go and gain clarity and direction toward a new start.

Philippians 4:7 speaks of God giving a peace that surpasses all understanding. Forgiveness may not appear as a simple thing to do. It may take time and plenty of tissue boxes, but you can do it! First you have to make a decision to be happy. Forgiving demonstrates that you are focused on your own personal growth. The only person you can change is yourself, so strive to be your best! Acceptance and forgiveness work together in order to gain peace and joy.

The next step is to be thankful. Focus on the positive rather than the negative things in your life. Life itself is enough to be thankful for. It may seem easier to dwell on everything that is going wrong, but why? Is that going to make it any better? No. Instead, choose to be thankful for all that you have, whether it's your family, friends, job, house, or just keeping your sanity! The key is to stay positive and motivated.

A Woman's Beauty

Women critique the way you think and live, study your lives
Are you demonstrating your inner beauty or flashing hidden
secrets and lies?
The depth of conversation suggesting betrayal
Of your dignity, self worth and passion to prevail
Don't you know the great value of a women's strength, all that
we do?
Don't neglect Gods crafted gifts he specifically placed in you
Embrace the magnificent intense fragrance of a woman's pride
Breathe breaths of emotion, success, elegance and stride
For we set the assuaging tone for calmness and peace
Our charisma, like a sweet sensual aroma to release
The essence of a woman like a vivacious rhythm as soft as lace
Let your beauty shine bright with class, wisdom and grace

It's All About You!

Time to live your life and be happy! Let's start off by having a reason to smile. Laughter is therapeutic. After going through everything you have gone through, do you know when you are truly over it? When you can sit back, reminisce about it all, and laugh! When I think of some of the ridiculous things I did in the heat of the moment when dealing with drama, I am glad that I can finally laugh about it! At that very moment, it was far from funny. It's a great feeling to redirect your focus back on the one person who deserves it: *you!*

Embrace the new you and expect good things to come your way. It's important to set priorities to keep yourself focused and motivated. There are seven areas in your life I suggest you set goals for in order to maintain balance.

1. **Family**. Focus on building and maintaining healthy relationships with your family. Family is so important and at times is all we have. When I went through my own personal despair, I isolated myself from all of my family and friends. I was angry and disappointed with the failure of my relationship. It made me withdraw from everyone because of fear to have to explain my situation; I just didn't want

to talk about it. Looking back, that is the last thing you want to do. You need your family for support. Family is not limited to blood ties. You may have friends who you are just as connected to. Value each moment you spend, and build lasting relationships with the ones you love.

2. **Personal**. Sometimes, you just need some *me* time! Go to the spa, get your nails done, or listen to some music. At times, you have to learn to be your own best friend. Enjoy spending time with yourself! Relax, and unwind. I will never forget the time one of my best friends told me how she used to go to the movies alone. I thought, incredulous that I would ever be that desperate, *How can you go alone?* Silly me. One night, I tried, and it felt great! I love having me time. :-) (That's a smiley face for all you non-texters!) Once you are comfortable and happy with the person you are and the person you are becoming, others will be comfortable too. If you do not even like being with you, why would others? Love the skin you're in. You are unique, valuable, and worth all the best life has to give.

3. **Physical**. Staying fit and eating healthy affect how you look and feel. When you look good, you feel

good about yourself. When you feel good about yourself, you are likely to be happier and easier to be around. Plus going to the gym is a great way to meet people, but we will get to that later! I suggest setting realistic goals for diet and exercise. Try not to overdo it.

4. **Spiritual**. For me, it's taking time to pray and seek God for direction, protection, and peace. I am a believer that God answers prayers. I seek to be in tune with what God is doing in my life so that I am moving in the right direction. Knowing that he is there to guide me, has given me a sense of comfort and peace. An excellent prayer to say each day is in Joel Osteen's "Your Best Life Now Journal." *"Heavenly father you have given me eyes to see and a mind to search for wisdom. Today I ask that you open the eyes of my heart and my mind to see myself as you see me-blessed, loved, and full of joy! Help me to envision the dreams I've pushed aside, to see myself accepting and living out what you desire in my life."*

Having purpose and spiritual peace is a major goal I set in this area.

5. **Mental**. Mentally, I always want to be developing as an individual. No matter how old you are, you are never too old to learn something new. Reading (as in what you are doing now) is a great way to stimulate your mind. Ever heard the saying "If you don't use it, you lose it"? I encourage you to always challenge yourself. You'd be surprised what you're capable of doing.

6. **Career and finances**. I strive to be the best at whatever endeavor I pursue. Setting goals for career advancement may mean going back to school to get a degree in a particular area. It is equally important to prioritize your finances. Working toward financial stability requires discipline. Money management is a major area that affects all of our lives. This is also an area that can make or break a relationship. The route of many couples' issues usually stems from frustration with finances. Money issues can lead to resentment and stress. A great ultimate goal to consider is making your money work for you rather than you constantly working for your money! There are so many different legal ways to accumulate money rather than working endless hours and not reaping the full benefits of your labor.

I went to a workshop once that discussed having multiple streams of income. The main three areas were core, passive, and passion income. Your core income is your main job. This is how you pay all your bills, such as rent, mortgage, and utilities. The passive income is created through investing, such as in stocks and 401(k). Passion income is income coming in by doing something you have a passion to do. You may love to cook so you start a business selling pies. You may like to knit sweaters or even sell cars. Whatever you enjoy, doing that will generate additional income.

7. **Social**. It's great to have a social life! I love great conversation and being around different personalities. Networking, building relationships, will be helpful in the long run. I think it's important to build meaningful friendships; they usually last a lifetime.

    When socializing, be aware of who you allow into your space. When trying to set a tone in your life for positive energy, watch out for negative, unhappy people. They will try to depress you and kill your dreams. **Surround yourself with people who are**

uplifting and will help nurture your progress. Sometimes, even certain family members you have to limit time with in order to stay focused on being a better you.

A Clear Vision

Extravagant frames magnify shades to a person's vision
Look at them and see that their purpose is such a message
Take a look at someone's thoughts and view a hidden blessing
Reality is consequences to our deepest fears
Life's pulsating vibrations persuade the puddles of our tears
Don't be deceived by illusions that make you think that you're not
Grab your destiny, dream big and envision a greater plot

Taking Control of Your Destiny

It's time to focus on being your best. Joel Osteen's book *Become a Better You* states, "One of the most important keys to a better life is to keep yourself happy, rather than living to please everyone else." Sounds simple enough, right? Make yourself a priority! No, this does not mean you should be selfish. Instead, it suggests we do not cause ourselves to suffer at the extent of someone else's happiness. If you are a people pleaser, this is especially for you!

I have an exercise for you to try. Open your mouth, stand up straight, and let the word *no* roll passionately off your tongue. There you go. Now try it again! I think you have mastered the technique of saying no. Sometimes, it is necessary. It may be the hardest task to overcome, but sometimes, you have to tell people no. It's important to be generous and kind whenever you have the opportunity, but what I'm implying is to not be so selfless that you are constantly neglecting yourself. It is okay to have happiness in your life. Welcome it, and embrace it.

Now let's focus on your pursuit for happiness. What do you enjoy doing? Dina Beauvais, the author of *Dreams to Destiny,* encourages the use of your talents and gifts to do what you have a **healthy passion** to do. She recommends pursuing goals that are within your niche, which are areas of "your highest and best use." In her book, she says, "*Maybe your unique purpose or niche in life is to be an excellent stay-at-home mom? Maybe it's to be a great teacher, a skilled carpenter, cook or CEO? Perhaps it's to be an artist, architect or athlete. It doesn't matter. Not everyone is an entrepreneur and it's not about becoming a millionaire. What's important is that you discover your true dreams and passions and connect them with the gifts and talents you were given at birth. In this way you will discover who you are designed to be. Then you can step into your divine destiny*".

An excellent example would be that writing is my labor of love. Growing up, it was something that I always enjoyed doing without even being told to do it. I would write poems, short stories and scribbled endless personal entries in my journals. It was a gift that family and friends also complimented me on. I even took a creative writing class in order to develop it. It is difficult to experience self-fulfillment if your heart is not in all that you are doing and represent. **Once you are engaging in activities that bring you fulfillment and purpose, you are less likely to go blindly searching for satisfaction and purpose through someone else**.

"You were meant for greatness, not mediocrity," Beauvais wrote. We are all capable of achieving superlative success. God has blessed us all with gifts and talents. Activate and develop them in order to reach your full potential.

A New Start

Now that you are more vibrant, liberated, and looking and feeling great, are you ready to give love another chance? I know you probably have this long list of characteristics for the ideal man. You're like, "I'm not settling, it's time to imagine the mysterious Mr. Right!" This is an exhilarating yet apprehensive transition. You are going from letting go of strong, unsettling emotions to being in pursuit of giving and receiving love and affection.

A major element in the process of letting go is leaving all that distrust and rejection in the past. This will be a fresh start. You are not the ambassador of heartbreak. So the key is to leave all the negative thinking and view a new beginning. How do you let go of the negativity? By envisioning how good it will make you feel! It's like a burden has been lifted off of you. Wouldn't it be great to trust, love, respect, and honor your man? This is the foundation that you want to build for your new relationship. Base it on new experiences and feelings. Let go of the past and create the relationship you desire.

Reflect on yourself. Do you fit the criteria of what you expect from your future man? I know in an earlier chapter I said it's all about you, but that is true to an extent. A relationship is about coming together to add and complement each other's lives. It's not about what one person can offer. What are you both bringing to the table? There are people who are only looking out for themselves and have different arrangements or agreements, and that's their preference. I believe building a healthy foundation requires a mutual trust and respect.

It's so easy to put expectations on others. At times we have to set standards for ourselves as well. For example, if you are adamant on attracting someone who works out and is fit, shouldn't you take the initiative to make sure your body is right too? Whether its physical or emotional, it's important to make sure that both of you want to please each other. Don't you want your partner to be as fulfilled and connected to you as you are with them? You have to learn how to love right. An element of that is by reciprocating what is being given to you. This will all make sense once you have determined this is a relationship worth investing in.

1 Corinthians 13:4 "Love is patient, love is kind, and it is not jealous, love does not brag and is not arrogant." Love is a beautiful, giving, selfless emotion that when expressed correctly and to one deserving, can bring great joy, peace, and happiness. Most importantly, love should not hurt! In order to gain love, it has to first begin with you loving yourself. Now that you have gone through the storm, healed, and become a better you, don't be afraid to dust yourself off and try again. Be willing to love freely, without regrets.

You live,

and you learn.

When I Say

When I say I love you I mean I love the way you are
Past your flaws your smile reaches far
When I say I'll give you my all I mean all of my heart
Presenting my love as a gift take it and treat it with care
Extend you love to me as a stream of constant pure affection
Bringing light to a dim room
Highlighting the rough stepping stones leading to my heart
Gently massaging the sharp edges where I had to break off past
pain that tried to wear me down
Now I'm free
Look
See deep within my essence
The Amber Brown moonlight sparkle in my eyes
Faint but familiar
That passionate glow took time to reignite but you strong voice,
nurturing touch and warm words of promise enkindled a
lifeline of love
I can feel
When I say this feels right
I mean after experiencing moments of failed attempts at sincerity
I found what's real when you lovingly spoke my name
When you tenderly grabbed my hand and serenaded me with
a melody of trust that left a tattoo along the depth of my soul
You own this
This is real
When I say thank you I mean Thank you

I mean thank you for allowing me to know what it feels like to trust, to believe to envision all I ever wanted and needed God created when he made you
When I say you have my heart
I mean I Love the piece of yours you've given to me
Gift wrapping love and devotion, a timeless treasure that I hold as sacred as the secrets we share
Our united essence abandoning any lonely moments of despair
Allowing past emotions to fade away and disappear
I see why I needed you the most before we even met
I knew I was waiting for this feeling of completeness I hadn't experienced yet
When I say I know you, I mean you know me
We are a reflection of each other, a mirror of our inner self
You understand me better than most, we are connected beyond an explanation
Joined as one, a promised bond without any original relation
But definitely meant to be this is so true
It only makes sense to be linked, you with me, I with you

Afterword

Abuse

In the book, I briefly spoke on verbal and physical abuse when this is actually a critical topic to discuss. In no way should anyone accept the circumstances in an abusive relationship. There are so many support groups and avenues that are directly related to the destruction of this type of behavior. But it all boils down to you and your tolerance. Low self-esteem is a poison that clouds your vision and disfigures your actual self-perception. Feelings of worthlessness and shame may shield malicious actions. Realizing your value is essential to gaining self-respect.

Each and every life is precious. Once someone begins to treat themselves with reverence, then that is what they will eventually only accept. If you or someone you know needs help in getting out of an abusive relationship, seek a trusted pastor, family member, or local support group immediately! Save a life! There is nothing to be ashamed of. The victory is overcoming! You live and you learn.

What about the children?

In part 2, we discussed how our actions can affect our own lives, but what if there are children involved? Children are always watching what we do. If you are on the wrong path in the journey of life, constantly taking the wrong turns going into dead-end streets, then you are causing you children to be off course as well. When there is balance in your life, your children reap the benefits. When you are where you need to be, you are in a position to be an effective parent, giving clear instruction. One of the things I always feared was messing up my children's lives because of the decisions I made, allowing them to be in an environment that would affect them emotionally and cause them to act out later in life. There are so many people with emotional issues that stem back to childhood experiences that they don't even remember! No one is perfect, but be aware of what you expose your children to.

Happily Ever After

Do you believe in "happily ever after"? I do. Although the divorce rate is not favorable of this, I still believe that love conquers all. I think that the ingredient to a lasting relationship is focusing on the positive, envisioning nothing but success. This is more effective when you know a successful relationship to reflect on. I'm not suggesting you imitate another couple, but use them as a visual. They will be your proof that real love does exist.

Now in the book, I gave examples of celebrities, but you can focus on regular, everyday couples that you may know. One of the most influential couples I have ever known was my bishop, Joseph Norfleet, and his wife, Lady Madeline Norfleet. Their love for each other is so genuine and inspiring. They support one another, and their personalities definitely balance each other out! When it's meant to be, a connection of love, trust, and devotion, makes a successful relationship more attainable.

I Would Love to Hear from You!

One of the reasons for writing this book was to connect with women all over the world and share a theme of hope and encouragement. No one is exempt from dealing with different issues in life, whether with a spouse, friend, or family member. I just want to let you all know that we are all connected! This is a sisterhood of support. We are all meant for greatness!

An awarding incentive in presenting this book is being able to connect with total strangers and talk about life! I want to encourage women to build one another up, not break each other down. I would love to hear your perspectives and experiences on love and relationships. Let me know any questions you may have. Contact me however you would like.

E-mail   ambershanel0103@gmail.com

Facebook @ambershanel

Instagram @brownsugar28

I would love to get to know my readers and have some great girl talk!